The PINK HOUSE

TARNISHA HARPER-PHILLIPS

The
PINK
HOUSE

Once upon a time there was a little brown girl who lived in a pink house.

The little brown girl, who lived in the pink house, stared out of her room window at the top of the pink house.

Books

The little brown girl, who lived in the pink house, who stared out of the window, watched the cars go by.

The little brown girl, who lived in the pink house, who watched the cars go, by daydreamed at the moon at night.

The little brown girl, who
lived in the pink house,
who daydreamed at the
moon at night, imagined
that she could fly.

The little brown girl who
lived in the pink house
who imagined that she
could fly closed her
eyes listening to the
sounds of the outside.

The little brown girl who lived in the pink house who closed her eyes listening to the sounds of outside heard birds chirping, kids laughing, adults talking and music playing.

The little brown girl who
lived in the pink house who
heard the birds chirping,
kids laughing adults
talking and music started
dancing to the sounds
of the music playing.

The little brown girl who
lived in the pink house who
started dancing to the
sound of the music twirled
in her room spinning
around and around.

The little brown girl
who lived in the pink
house who twirled in her
room spinning around
and around imagined she
was a princess wearing
a beautiful pink dress.

The little brown girl who
lived in the pink house
who imagined she was
a princess wearing a
beautiful pink dress placed
the crown on her head.

The little brown girl who lived in the pink house who placed the crown on her head sat on her throne.

The little brown girl who
lived in the pink house
who sat on her throne
smiled at all the other
children around her.

The little brown girl who
lived in the pink house
who smiled at all the
other children around
her heard her name
being called from afar.

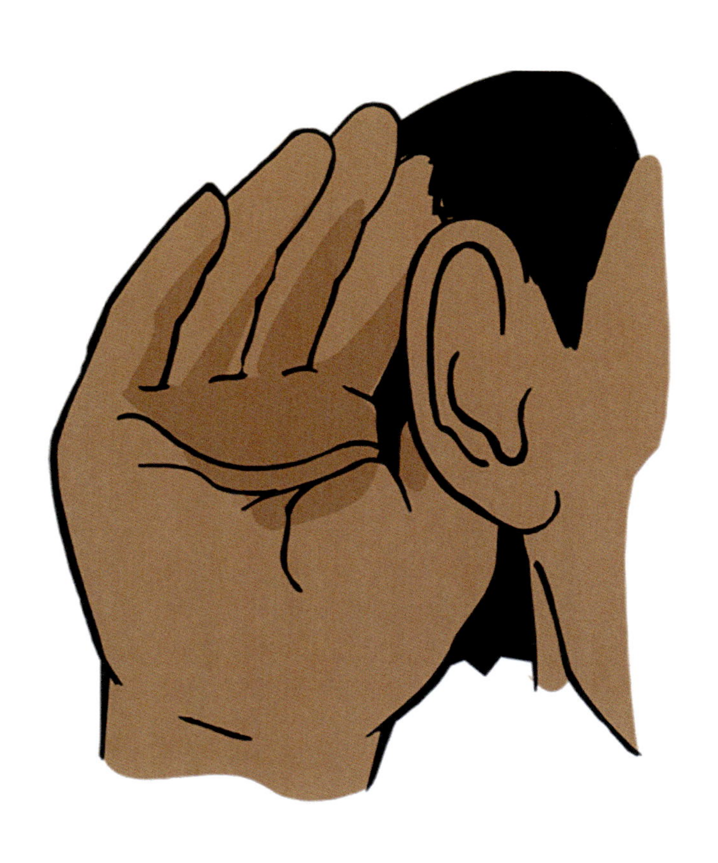

The little brown girl, who lived in the pink house, who heard her name being called from afar, opened her eyes and realized that it was her mother.

Mother

The little brown girl who
lived in the pink house
who opened her eyes
and realized that her
mother was calling her
ran down the stairs.

The little brown girl who
lived in the pink house
who ran down the stairs
was surprised by her
entire family screaming
happy birthday to her.

The little brown girl, who
lived in the pink house,
was so shocked by the
surprise that she started
crying with tears of joy.

The little brown girl, who lived in the pink house, who was shocked by the surprise and cried with tears of joy. realized she was already a princess.

Princess

The little brown girl, who lived in the pink house, who realized that she was already a princess, imagined and all her dreams came true with all the things she already had.

The little brown girl,
who lived in the pink
house, was a princess
dressed in a pink gown
with a crown on her
head. She looked out the
window at the top of her
pink house and listened
to the birds chirping;
the cars going by;

the music playing; the kids laughing; and adults talking while the little brown girl was dancing to the music, twirling in her room, imagining she could fly. The glistening moon smiled at the stars and shouted GOOD NIGHT!!!!!!!

The

End???

What color is your house?

What do you daydream about?

When is your birthday?

Draw the members
of your family.

This book is dedicated to all the little brown girls who often daydream of things they want to become and the places they want to see.

All it takes is a little
imagination, some pictures
and some words to make
your dreams come true.
Be thankful for your
family and the things
you have around you;
cherish them and, most
importantly, love yourself.

This book is dedicated to my grandmother Verna Mae Harper. Without her there would be no pink house filled with love and little brown children!!

Made in the USA
Middletown, DE
17 March 2024

51666920R00033